C#

The Ultimate Beginners Guide to C# Programming

Table of Contents

Introduction

I want to thank you and congratulate you for purchasing the book, "C#".

This book contains proven steps and strategies on how to write codes using the C# language.

This eBook will teach you the basics of C# programming. It will explain the different aspects of C#, such as methods, classes, and variables. The ideas and techniques that you'll find in this book can boost your overall programming skills.

This material contains concise definitions, detailed instructions, and actual codes. You don't have to worry if you have never created a program before. With this book, you will be writing your own programs in no time.

Thanks again for downloading this book, I hope you enjoy it!

Chapter 1: The Basics of C#

Programming Languages

A computer application consists of commands that follow a specific sequence. Each sequence of commands aims to complete a particular task. As a programmer, you'll type these commands on a text file. Once done, the text file will serve as the "source code" of your program. You have to follow strict rules when creating a program - even a single mistake can cause runtime problems. Fortunately, there are many programming languages that you can choose from.

Basically, programming languages give you clear rules for writing your own codes. There are various programming languages out there. Each computer language has its own pros and cons. In this book, you'll learn about the C# language. C# is one of the most popular languages today.

Compilation

Keep in mind that you have to store your codes (also known as "statements") in a text file. That means your program is just a document that contains various commands. These commands consist of characters that are not compatible with computers. Thus, you have to "translate" your commands into a language that computers can understand. Programmers refer to the "translation" process as "compilation".

During compilation, the "compiler" (i.e. the tool that translates your code) will check your source code for errors. The process will stop if there is an error in your code. The compiler will require you to correct the mistake before

4

continuing the compilation process. This is a useful feature. It can help you in detecting and solving issues present in your programs. Unfortunately, the compiler cannot identify all kinds of mistakes. It is possible for a compiled program to contain one or more errors.

Programming is more than just typing codes. It requires you to use statements in solving problems or completing tasks. The process of completing tasks through a computer language is known as creating an "algorithm". Thus, programming involves the creation of various algorithms.

The Tools You Need

You need a text editor to write a program. Most beginners opt for Notepad, the default text editor of Windows computers. However, you can save your time if you will use an IDE (i.e. integrated development environment). If you are a Windows user, you may use Visual Studio, a powerful programming tool from Microsoft. Visual Studio comes with all the programs you'll need in creating C#-based computer applications.

Important Note: You can't use word processors (e.g. Microsoft Word) when writing codes. That's because word processors automatically use special format and characters to whatever you type. Some of these formats and characters are not compatible with language compilers. If you want risk-free programming, just use Notepad or your chosen IDE.

Object-Oriented Programming

Like many programming languages, C# is object-oriented. That means C# relies on objects that resemble the things we see in the real world. The most basic part of a computer application is called "class". Classes define the functions and attributes of the program they belong to. As a programmer, you should remember that each program is a collection of classes. Also, everything that you'll do with the C# language involves at least one class. Your program will likely operate using classes that were created by other people. These "external classes" are available in the framework called ".NET".

How to Add Comments

In programming, a comment is a sentence or a block of text that provides additional information. A comment doesn't affect the function or behavior of the program itself. Thus, you can use comments to insert reminders inside your application. This way, you won't forget important data regarding the projects you work on. Comments are extremely useful - they can help you understand codes you wrote many years ago.

To create a comment in C#, you may use one of these symbols:

- // - This symbol is designed for single-line comments.
- /* */ - Use this symbol for comments that span multiple lines.

Your First Computer Program

Every program should have a starting class. That class marks the point where the program will start running. C# requires a specific syntax when naming a program's "starting point". Nothing beats first-hand experience, so let's go ahead and create your first program. The example given below, despite its simplicity, will show you the most basic parts of a C# program. Launch your favorite text editor and type the following code;

```
using System;
Namespace FirstProgram
{
        class Sample
        {
                static void Main(string[] args)
                {
                        Console.WriteLine("I'm awesome.");
                }
        }
}
```

This program will open a command prompt and display the following message:

"I'm awesome."

Now, let's create the same program using Visual Studio:

1. Launch the development tool and click on "File".
2. Hit "New" and choose "Project".
3. Make sure that the language is set to "C#".
4. The screen will show you various types of programs. Select "Console Application".
5. Specify the location where you want to save the program's source code. (You can keep things simple by choosing "Desktop").
6. Specify the name of the program. For this example, type "FirstProgram".
7. Hit "Ok" or press the Enter key of your keyboard. The programming tool will generate a template for your new program. The template should look like this:

```csharp
using System;
using System.Collections.Generic;
using System.Linq;
using System.Text;
using System.Threading.Tasks;

namespace FirstProgram
{
        class Sample
        {
                static void Main(string[] args)
                {
                }
        }
}
```

The code in the image creates a "live" program. You may execute it on your computer. It won't generate any problems, but it won't do anything either. To make the program display a message, insert the following statement into the code:

Console.WriteLine("I'm awesome.");

Put that statement between the last pair of parentheses (i.e. right under the "static..." line).

Now, click on the "Debug" option of Visual Studio and launch the program without debugging. The screen should show you the "I'm awesome." message.

Analyzing the Program

The code has uppercase and lowercase letters. Keep in mind that the C# language is case-sensitive. If you aren't careful with letter capitalization, your programs might encounter fatal errors during compilation or runtime.

C# applications have various classes. In this example, the name of the class is "Sample". Each class contains methods and variables. The current example contains one method

8

named "Main()". The Main() method serves as the starting point of the program. Methods hold commands that a computer can perform. Invoking a method means running the statements inside that method. Two words precede the "Main()" method: static and void. You'll know the purpose of those words later.

The Main() method holds the WriteLine() statement. Basically, WriteLine() is a method that prints data on your screen. This method belongs to the "Console" class (i.e. one of the built-in classes of the C# language).

In the C# language, classes are divided into different namespaces. The namespace called "System" holds many classes (e.g. the "Console" class). The name of a class consists of three parts: (1) the namespace it belongs to, (2) a period, and (3) the name of the class itself (e.g. System.Console). You can use the "using" command to simplify your codes. With this command, you won't have to specify the namespace of your classes. You can just type the name of the class you want to use. For example, you can just type *Console.WriteLine("C# is great.");* instead of *System.Console.WriteLine("C# is great.");*

Important Note: You should terminate each command using a semicolon. That symbol helps the C# compiler in identifying the end of your commands.

More Information

The Visual Studio IDE stores applications in their own namespaces. For this example, Visual Studio saved the program in a namespace called "FirstProgram". But specifying the "FirstProgram" namespace is not necessary if you used a text editor. In fact, the codes become much simpler if you are using a basic text editor like Notepad. Let's use another example:

1. Access your favorite text editor.
2. Type the following:

```
class SecondProgram
{
        static void Main()
        {
                System.Console.WriteLine("I am happy.");
        }
}
```

3. Save the file as "SecondProgram.cs". The text file will serve as the source code of your new program.
4. It's time to compile the source code. Launch a command prompt and type "csc SecondProgram.cs".
5. The compiler will generate an ".exe" file. You can run the resulting file by double-clicking it.

Important Note: To keep this material simple, the succeeding chapters will assume that you are using Visual Studio. If you don't have that software yet, you may go online and download it first.

Chapter 2: The Structure of C# Programs

The example given in the previous chapter shows the basic structure of C# programs. As mentioned earlier, the Main() method serves as the starting point of every program written using C#. In the current chapter, you will create a program that contains multiple statements. This chapter will also teach you how to use C# methods.

Writing the Program

Your objective is to create a computer application that displays data about a person.

The Process

1. Launch Visual Studio and create a new project.
2. Set "C#" as the programming language and select "Console Application".
3. Set "ThirdProgram" as the name of the project and hit "OK".
4. You will see a program outline on the screen. Change the outline so that it looks like this:

```
using System;
namespace ThirdProgram
{
        class Sample
        {
                static void Main(string[] args)
                {
                        Name();
                        Achievements();
                }
```

```
        }

        private static void Name()
        {

                Console.WriteLine("Magnus Carlsen");
                Console.WriteLine("The Mozart of
Chess");

        }

        private static void Achievements()
        {

                Console.WriteLine("Highest Elo in
History");
                Console.WriteLine("World Chess
Champion since 2013");
        }
    }
}
```

5. Run the program after compiling it. If you did everything right, you should see the following message on your screen:

Magnus Carlsen
The Mozart of Chess
Highest Elo in History
World Chess Champion since 2013

Analyzing the Program

This program has a lot of similarities with the previous ones. It simply prints some text on the screen. The main difference, however, is that the messages exist in newly created methods. Based on this example, the syntax of C# methods is:

```
private static void NameofMethod()
{

// The statements you want to run.

}
```

For instance, the current example has two new methods (i.e. "Name()" and "Achievements()"). Each method has a name followed by a pair of parentheses. You can invoke a method by specifying its name. Once you run this new program, Main() will trigger the Name() and Achievements() methods. Thus, the messages they contain will appear on your screen.

More Information

Visual Studio generates various files and directories for each of your projects. The name of the directory is the same as that of the project itself. The directory holds various files related to the project. For console applications, however, you should focus on two files: (1) the source code, and (2) the compiled program. The source code of the program has the ".cs" extension. You can find it in the main directory of your project. To find the compiled program, you should click on "bin" and "Debug". The finished product has the ".exe" extension. You may transfer that extension to another directory or computer.

Chapter 3: The Variables of the C# Language

Computer programs have to process information. And information processing requires a tool for storing the results. In C#, you can use variables to store information within your programs. Each variable has a type, a name, and one or more operators.

You can use the name of the variable for reference and identification purposes. Like most programming languages, C# is lenient when it comes to variable names. There are three rules concerning variable names. These rules are:

- Each variable name should begin with a lowercase letter
- You may use numbers and letters to complete the name
- Spaces are now allowed

The variable's type determines the kind of information that you can store inside that variable. The type of the variable also specifies the types of operations that are compatible with that variable. In the C# language, you have to declare a variable before using it. The syntax for variable declaration is:

datatype nameofvariable = thevalue;

You should specify the data type of the variable. Then, give the variable's name and the value you want to store. For instance:

int sample = 100;

The statement given above generates a variable named "sample" that belongs to the "int" type. The initial value of that variable is 100.

Important Note: You should always declare a variable before using it. Undeclared variables can cause errors during compilation.

The following list shows the built-in data types of C#:

- int - With this type, you can store 32-bit signed integers.
- uint - This data type is for 32-bit unsigned integers.
- char - Use this type for 16-bit Unicode characters.
- bool - Use this data type for Boolean values.
- short - This type can store 16-bit signed integers.
- ushort - With this data type, you can store 16-bit unsigned integers.
- byte - Use this type for 8-bit signed integers.
- sbyte - This data type is designed for 8-bit unsigned integers.
- string - This is the data type for text or character strings.
- decimal - Use this type for 96-bit decimal numbers.
- double - The "double" type is created for 64-bit floating-point values.
- float - With the float type, you can store 32-bit floating-point values.
- ulong - Use this type for unsigned 64-bit unsigned integers.
- long - This is the data type for 64-bit signed integers.

Let's discuss the data types with the help of a basic example. Create another project in Visual Studio and name it "FourthProgram". The rest of the settings should be similar to those of previous examples. Edit the resulting structure so that it looks like this:

```
using System;

namespace FourthProgram
{
        class Sample
        {
                static void Main()
                {
                        uint firstnumber = 100;
                        uint secondnumber = 50;
                        uint difference = firstnumber -
secondnumber;
                        Console.WriteLine("Deducting " +
secondnumber + " from " + firstnumber " gives you " +
difference);
                }
        }
}
```

Compile the program and run it. If you did everything right, a command prompt will appear and display the following:

Deducting 50 from 100 gives you 50

Analyzing the Program

This program generates two uint variables and names them "firstnumber" and "secondnumber". The initial value of "firstnumber" is 100 while that of "secondnumber" is 50. Because the declaration statements are inside the Main() method, the resulting variables are only accessible inside that method. Variables affected by this kind of limitation are known as "local variables". Then, the program creates a third variable and uses it to store the difference between the first two variables. That means the value of the third variable comes from a programming expression (i.e. firstnumber - secondnumber;). The WriteLine() command prints the information on your screen. As you can see, the sentence in the code consists of different segments joined by plus symbols. The plus symbol concatenates (or links) different values and converts them to strings.

The Operators

The C# language has many operators. These operators work on values or variables present in your codes. The previous example relied on "=", "-" and "+". Keep in mind that the function of an operator changes based on the operands (i.e. the values or variables) it works on. The programming expression for the "difference" variable is subtraction. The plus symbols in the WriteLine() command, however, trigger concatenation of strings. The program also used the equal sign to assign a value to a variable.

The list given below shows the operators present in C# language:

- Unary - x, ~, !, -, +, (T)x, --x, and ++x
- Additive - + and -
- Multiplicative - %, *, and /
- Shift - >> and <<
- Equality - != and =
- Primary - ~, --x, x.y, f(x), new, nameof, default, unchecked, typeof, checked, x++, x?.y, and a[x]
- Conditional OR - ||
- Conditional AND - &&
- Conditional - ?:
- Logical OR - |
- Logical AND - &&

- Logical XOR - ^
- Assignment - +=, -=, >>=, =>, <<=, |=, *=, %=, /=, ^=, and &=
- Null Coalescing - "??"

A unary operator is an operator that can work on a single value or variable. There are two major categories of C# unary operators: prefix and postfix. Analyze the examples below:

uint firstsample = 3;
uint secondsample = --firstsample;
uint thirdsample = 100;
uint fourthsample = thirdsample++;

If you will print the variable named "secondsample", you will get 2. That's because the operator will run before the WriteLine() method. Printing "fourthsample", on the other hand, gives you 100. The "++" operator will work on the variable after the WriteLine() method's execution.

Unary operators are easy to understand. The problems arise when you are dealing with expressions involving various values, variables, or operators. The precedence of mathematical operators also work in C#. If you are dealing with multiple operators, it would be best if you'll use parentheses to enclose segments of your expressions. This way, you can get the result that you need. Here's an example:

Instead of typing: "$x - y / z$", you may type: "$(x - y) / z$".

In the first expression, y will be divided by z because division has a higher priority than subtraction. If you want to subtract y from x before performing division, the second expression is ideal.

Most of the C# operators are intuitive. However, some can be confusing for beginners. Let's discuss the different types of assignment operators:

uint x = 99;
x += 1;

The code given above gives you 100. Basically, the first statement creates a variable named x and sets 99 as the initial value. The second statement, on the other hand, increases the value by one and assigns the resulting value to the same variable.

Chapter 4: Console Applications

This chapter will give you more information about console applications. Console applications are programs that require a terminal or command prompt. In this chapter, you'll know how programs obtain information from users and how output formatting works.

Writing the Program

In this exercise, you will create a program that asks for the user's name. Then, the program will display a greeting. Here are the steps:

1. Launch Visual Studio and create a new project.
2. Set "FifthProgram" as the name of this program.
3. Choose "C#" and "Console Application".
4. Hit "OK" and copy the following code:

```
using System;
namespace FifthProgram
{
        class Sample
        {
                static void Main(string[] args)
                {
                        Console.Write("What is your name: ");
                        string name = Console.ReadLine();
                        Console.WriteLine("Good morning, " + name + ("! How are you doing today?");
                }
        }
}
```

5. Execute the program after compiling it. If you did everything right, it should ask for your name and display a customized greeting.

Analyzing the Program

This program has a single Main() method and contains the structure found in previous examples. Basically, the program displays a text string and asks the user to provide data. Check the following statement:

Console.Write("What is your name: ");

The initial text appears thanks to the Write() method. Keep in mind that WriteLine and Write() are two different methods. WriteLine() adds a newline character after the displayed string. The Write() method, on the other hand, handles the text string as is.

The statement given below uses the ReadLine() method. Simply put, ReadLine() is a tool that you can use to obtain information from your users. Users can submit their answer using the Enter key. The answer will be stored as a text string. Remember that ReadLine() always produces string values. If you are dealing with numbers, you have to convert the user's entry to the proper number format.

Once the user enters his name, the program will store the value inside a variable called "name". Then, the program will display the greeting on a terminal and insert the name of the user.

A Time-and-Date Computer Program

Now, let's create a program that displays the current time and date (i.e. according to your computer). To complete this program, you have to:

- Create another Visual Studio project. You should name this one "SixthProgram".
- Use the settings from previous examples.
- Edit the body of the structure so that it looks like:

```
static void Main(string[] args)
{
        DateTime sample = DateTime.Now;
        Now(xy);

}

static void First(Now y)
{
        Console.WriteLine(t.ToLongTimeString());
        Console.WriteLine(t.ToLongDateString());
}
```

Analyzing the Program

In the first section of the code, the program stores the current time and date values of your computer. The said values will go to a variable named "xy". Here's the statement:

DateTime xy = DateTime.Now;

DateTime, one of the built-in classes of C#, contains various methods designed for time and date values. The "Now" section obtains the values from the clock of your computer.

The second code block, on the other hand, prints the information on your screen. That code block utilized built-in methods to format the value inside the variable. If you did everything properly, a command prompt should appear and display the current time and date of your computer.

Chapter 5: How to Control a Program's Flow

All of the programs you've created so far have a straightforward sequence. The statements will run according to their position in the source code. In the real world, however, your program should be able to behave or perform actions based on certain conditions. You can achieve this flexibility by adding control statements into your codes. In C#, you can use the following control statements:

- do
- if
- for
- while
- switch

Just like other statements, you can place a control statement in your methods. For instance, you can use a control statement in your ReadLine() or WriteLine() methods. Keep in mind, however, that conditional statements will perform an action only if the specified condition is met. You can use a conditional statement to run one or more commands. If you are dealing with multiple commands, you should place the commands inside a pair of brackets. Here is the syntax:

```
{

    firststatement;
    secondstatement;
    thirdstatement;
    ...
}
```

A code block can have many statements in it. In fact, you can place a block inside another block.

Let's discuss the conditional statements one by one:

The "if" Statement

The syntax of this conditional statement is:

if (your condition) codeblock

The condition part is an expression that gives a Boolean result (i.e. either "True" or "False"). If the expression results to "True", the program will run the commands you included in the conditional statement. If the result is "False", however, the program will skip the conditional commands. The basic program given below will show how "if" statements work:

1. Start another project using the Visual Studio environment.
2. Set the name of the project as "SeventhProgram".
3. Click on the OK button.
4. Delete the body of the resulting format and type:

```
static int Sample()
{
        Console.Write("Please give me a number: ");
        string ifvariable = Console.ReadLine();
        return Convert.ToInt32(ifvariable);
        int zz = 10;
}
```

The code given above asks the user to enter a number. The program, once finished, will say whether the number entered by the user is equal to 10. Here is the second part of the source code:

```
static void Sample1()
{
        if (ifvariable = zz)
        {
                Console.WriteLine("The number you entered is
equal to 10.");
        }
}
```

The sentence placed in the WriteLine method will appear if
the user's input is "10". If the user entered a different value,
the program will do nothing.

The "if-else" Statement

The "if-else" statement is more complex than the "if"
statement. With an if-else statement, you can run a default
command in case your conditional expression results to
"False". If the condition is satisfied, however, your preferred
command will run. The syntax of if-else statements is:

```
if (yourcondition)
        preferredblock
else
        defaultblock
```

Both of the code blocks (i.e. preferredblock and defaultblock)
can be basic C# commands. Keep in mind that the first block
will run if your condition is satisfied; otherwise, the second
block will. You can rewrite the previous example this way:

```
static void Sample()
{
        if (ifvariable = 10)
                Console.WriteLine("The number you entered is
equal to 10.");
```

```
        else
                Console.WriteLine("You entered an unknown
number.");

}
```

Important Note: With an if-else statement, you can control the flow of your program regardless of whether the condition is satisfied or not. That means if-else statements offer more control and flexibility than basic if statements.

The "while" Statements

Some situations require you to repeat a code block. Obviously, typing the same thing over and over again can be boring and time-consuming. Fortunately, C# offers the "while" statement. The syntax of this statement is:

```
while (yourcondition)
yourcodeblock
```

The code block (and all the statements inside it) will run while your condition is met. Once the result of the conditional expression becomes "False", the program will run the commands after your while loop. The example given below will help you understand how "while" loops work:

```
class Sample
{
        const int A = 100;
        static void Main(string[] args)
        {
                long x = 1;
                int a = 1;
                while (a <= A)
                {
```

```
            x += a;
        }
        Console.WriteLine(a);
    }
}
```

The third line of the code generates a constant named "A". This constant belongs to the "int" type and holds the value of 100. The sixth and seventh lines, on the other hand, declare two variables. The while statement in the eighth line utilizes the said variables in its conditional phrase. The value of "x" will be added to "a" until the latter becomes greater than or equal to "A". There is a WriteLine() method at the final section of the code. Thus, your command prompt should display the output of the program.

The "for" Statements

A "for" statement consists of three parts: (1) the initialization statement, (2) the condition, and (3) the default expression. Here is the syntax:

for (theinitialization; thecondition; theexpression)
block;

You have to separate the parts using semicolons. When you run a "for" statement, your program will:

- Run the initialization statement
- Check whether your condition is met
    - If the result of the second step is "True", the code block will run.
    - If the result is "False", the program will ignore the for statement's code block.
- Execute the default expression

28

- Repeat the second step

Important Note: The initialization, expression, and condition statements are completely optional. If you won't provide a conditional statement, the program will assume that the result is "True". Additionally, the code block may consist of a single statement.

Let's use a basic example:

```
static void Main(string[] args)
{
        int a = 1;
        for (int x = 2; x <= A; ++x) a += x;
        Console.WriteLine(a);
}
```

In this example, the "x" variable serves as a counter for the "for" statement. This variable counts the iterations conducted by the program. During each iteration, the statement given below runs:

```
a +=x;
```

Important Note: The value of the counter increases by one after each iteration. The process will continue until the counter's value becomes greater than or equal to that of "A".

The "do" Statements

A "do" statement is similar to a "while" statement. The syntax of "do" statements is:

```
do
{
firststatement;
```

secondstatement;
thirdstatement;
...
}
while (yourcondition);

As you can see, the condition is located at the final section of the syntax. Thus, your program will execute all of your codes first before checking whether your condition is met or not. If the condition is met, the process will start again. If the result is "False", the program will skip the "do" statement. The main benefit offered by a "do" statement is that your commands are guaranteed to run.

The "switch" Statements

You can use "switch" statements to choose specific data for your program. The example given below will illustrate this concept:

<u>Writing the Program</u>

```
static void Main(string[] args)
{
        Console.Write("Specify the month number: ");
        string variable1 = Console.ReadLine();
        switch (Convert.ToInt32(variable1))
        {
                case 1:
                        Console.WriteLine("January");
                        break;
                case 2:
                        Console.WriteLine("February");
                        break;
                case 3:
                        Console.WriteLine("March");
```

```
                    break;
          case 4:
                    Console.WriteLine("April");
                    break;
          case 5:
                    Console.WriteLine("May");
                    break;
          case 6:
                    Console.WriteLine("June");
                    break;
          case 7:
                    Console.WriteLine("July");
                    break;
          case 8:
                    Console.WriteLine("August");
                    break;
          case 9:
                    Console.WriteLine("September");
                    break;
          case 10:
                    Console.WriteLine("October");
                    break;
          case 11:
                    Console.WriteLine("November");
                    break;
          case 12:
                    Console.WriteLine("December");
                    break;
          default:
                    Console.WriteLine("You entered an
invalid number.");
                    break;
     }
}
```

Analyzing the Program

The fourth line of the code asks the user to provide a number. The number, which corresponds to a month, will be stored in a variable named "variable1". The code's fifth line will compare the value entered by the user with the cases inside the "switch" statement. If the user entered any number from 1 to 12, the name of the correct month will appear on the computer's screen. If the user will enter a number outside the said range, the program will return an error message.

Important Note: You don't have to place a default message for your switch statements.

Chapter 6: The Strings in the C# Language

In the C# language, strings are tools that you can use to represent text-based information. The characters inside a string belong to the "char" data type. Almost all programs involve strings. Thus, you have to be familiar with C# strings if you want to be a successful programmer.

Creating Strings

You can create string literals by placing one or more characters between a pair of double quotes. Here's an example:

string GM = "Kasparov";

Adding a special character in your strings is quite easy. You just have to use an "escape sequence". For instance:

string GM = "   \"Kasparov\"";

The C# language supports the following escape sequences:

- \v - Use this escape sequence to add a vertical tab.
- \t - This escape sequence allows you to insert a horizontal tab.
- \f - With this sequence, you can place a formfeed in your string literals.
- \a - Use this sequence to add an alert.
- \b - This sequence adds a backspace character in your string.

- \n - This sequence inserts a new line character in your string.
- \r - If you want to add a carriage return, this is the escape sequence you should use.
- \' - Use it to add a single quotation mark in your strings.
- \\ - With this sequence, you can add a normal backslash character.
- \0 - Use it to place a zero in your strings.
- \" - This is the sequence you must use to add double quotes in your strings.

You can refer to the characters of a string. For example, you can set the third character of a string as the initial value of a new variable. Here is the code:

```
string GM = "Kasparov";
char sample = GM[2];
```

You have to use an index to specify the character you want to use. In C#, the numbering of characters starts at zero. Thus, you need to type "2" if you want to use the third character.

String-Related Methods

C# provides various methods that you can use in handling or processing strings. Check the following code:

```
static void Main(string[] args)
{
        string sample = "KASPAROV";
        Console.WriteLine (sample);
        Console.WriteLine (sample.ToLower());
        Console.WriteLine (sample [4]);
        Console.WriteLine (sample.IndexOf ("PARO"));
```

```
        Console.WriteLine (sample.IndexOf ("PART"));
        Console.WriteLine (sample.Substring (3));
        Console.WriteLine (sample.Substring (1, 4));
        Console.WriteLine (sample.Length);
}
```

Analyzing the Code

The third line creates a variable named "sample". The initial
value of "sample" is "KASPAROV". The fourth line simply
prints the content of "sample" on the screen. The fifth line
displays the lowercase version of the string. The next line,
meanwhile, prints the fifth character of the string.

The IndexOf() method tells you where the initial occurrence
of your chosen substring is. Thus, the seventh line of the
code will give you "3". If you are looking for a non-existent
substring (like the eighth line of the code), you will get "-1".
The Substring() method divides the string based on your
parameter. If you will provide one parameter, your program
will display the string starting from your chosen element. If
you will give two arguments, the program will display the
characters between those two points. The ninth line has a
single parameter, so the program will print "PAROV". The
tenth line has two parameters, so your program will give you
"ASPAR". The eleventh line simply counts the characters
within the string.

Chapter 7: Arrays in C#

In programming, arrays are collections of objects. You can reference an array using its name. To reference an object inside an array, you have to specify the name of the array and the index number of that object. Remember that C# starts object numbering from zero. Thus, you should always use "0" when referring to the first object, "1" when referring to the second object, and so on.

Let's create a basic C# array:

int[] sample = new int[5];

The square brackets after "int" inform the C# compiler that you are creating an array. In this example, the array's name is "sample". The "new" keyword triggers the creation of the array. The number at the end of the code, however, specifies the array's capacity. It says "5", so the "sample" array can hold up to five objects. Keep in mind that this array belongs to the "int" data type. Thus, it can only accept numeric values.

For now, let's fill the array with different numbers:

sample[0] = 3;
sample[1] = 6;
sample[2] = 9;
sample[3] = 12;
sample[4] = 15;

The code given above uses the assignment operator (i.e. =) to place values inside the array. When assigning a value, you must indicate the name of the array and the location you want to work on. After assigning the values, you may use the array's contents in performing other C# operations.

String Arrays

C# arrays are flexible - they can hold numbers and letters. Thus, you can use an array to store different text strings. The following code will show you show:

```
static void Main(string[] args)
{
        string[] chesspieces = new string[6];
        chesspieces [0] = "Pawn";
        chesspieces [1] = "Knight";
        chesspieces [2] = "Bishop";
        chesspieces [3] = "Rook";
        chesspieces [4] = "Queen";
        chesspieces [5] = "King";
}
```

Important Note: You don't have to fill your arrays with values. If a value is missing, C# will consider that value as "null". Null values appear as blank spaces when printed on the screen.

Chapter 8: Object-Oriented Programming

A program won't function properly if it cannot handle data. That is why you must store data in one or more variables. Variables allow you to store and represent information easily. The C# language offers built in variable types. You can create complex programs without creating your own variables.

Sometimes, however, the built-in data types of C# don't meet your needs. Fortunately, you can utilize classes in your programs. Classes are programming tools that describe an object or concept inside a certain part of a computer application. There are ongoing debates regarding the true nature of classes. But to keep things simple, you may think of classes as typical data types. Unlike ordinary types, however, classes allow you to specify the appearance and functionality of the information you are dealing with.

If a variable belongs to the "class" data type, it is considered as an object. Objects are almost identical to ordinary variables. At this point, let's discuss how your computer allocates memory to objects and variables:

Memory Allocation

Active programs require a stack, a part of the computer's memory where variables are stored. In general, stacks allow programs to create and/or remove variables as needed. Computer stacks behave like stacks of cards. New variables are placed at the uppermost section of the computer stack. Thus, you can find the oldest variables at the bottom of the stack. The variables of basic data types (e.g. char, int, float, etc.) have identical sizes. The language compiler knows the size required by typical variables. That is the reason why such variables go straight to the stack.

The memory allocation for objects is more complex than the process outlined above. For starters, you have to use the "new" keyword when creating an object. Let's say you are working with a class called "Champions" and you need to generate an object inside it. The code that you should write is:

Champions Botvinnik = new Champion();

This syntax is similar to that of variable declaration. The name of the object is "Botvinnik". When you execute the "new" command, an object that belongs to the "Champions" type appears on the computer's "heap". Basically, the heap is the available memory that your computer can use. A variable will appear at the top of the stack, but that variable doesn't hold an actual value. Rather, it simply points to the new object. This is the reason why programmers refer to objects as "reference types".

Variables versus Objects

In general, variables that belong to the "value" type have greater efficiency than "reference" objects. But there are situations where reference objects are more effective than value variables. You should remember the processes outlined above because computer programs rely on the computer's heap and stack. Variables and objects have complex characteristics - you can do your own research after reading this book. For now, it is sufficient to know how computers allocate memory to the said programming tools.

C# Classes

The program below explains how C# classes work. You will create a basic program - one that conducts character pairing. This program will generate pairs of letters until the entries show "XX". Here are the things you should do:

- Create a data type that can represent the entries. Each entry has two possible forms: uppercase or lowercase. Let's name the data type "Character".
- Type the following code:

```
class Sample
{
        static void Main(string[] args)
        {
                Gene character1 = new Character();
                Gene character2 = new Character();
                do
                {
                        gene1.Throw();
                        gene2.Throw;
                        Console.WriteLine
(character1.SampleValue + " " + character2.SampleValue);
                }
                while (character1.SampleValue != 'X' ||
character2.SampleValue != 'X' );
        }
}

public class Character
{
        private static Random randomizer = new Random();
        private char samplevalue;

        public Character()
        {
```

40

```
                Throw();
        }
        public char SampleValue
        {
                get { return samplevalue; }
        }
        public void Throw()
        {
                samplevalue = (randomizer.Next(2) == 0) ? 'X'
: 'x';
        }
        public override string ToString()
        {
                return "" + samplevalue;
        }
}
```

Analyzing the Program

The program works by assuming that a character exists. You
can represent the imaginary character using a class called
"Character". As you can see, the Character class doesn't have
a Main() method. Also, the methods inside the class are not
"static". Classes are data types (or concepts) that you can
utilize in your programs.

In the C# language, classes have four parts:

- methods
- constructors
- properties
- instance variables

You can find all of these parts in the Character class given
above. There are two variables in that class: "randomizer"
and "samplevalue". The former belongs to the "Random"
data type. The latter, meanwhile, is a "char" variable. These

variables are tagged as "private". A private variable can only be accessed inside the class that contains it.

The Character class also has a Throw() method. When you run this method, a random form of the "X" character will appear. In addition, your program will store the resulting value in the variable called "samplevalue". You achieve this goal using "?", a C# operator that uses the following syntax:

yourcondition ? firstexpression : secondexpression;

Random is one of the built-in classes of C#. Just like other classes, Random has various methods that you can use. The program given above uses the "Next()" method, which generates a random non-negative number. When specifying a parameter for Next(), the number you will enter will be decreased by 1. Then, the method will generate a number from 0 to N (where N is the difference between your number and 1). In this case, the code for the program is:

randomizer.Next(2)

2 - 1 is 1, which means Next will give you either 1 or 0. The resulting value will go to the samplevalue variable.

Keep in mind that samplevalue, the program's member variable, is private. You cannot use it outside the Character class. Your program should know the values inside your member variable. You satisfy this requirement by setting the property of Character. Here is the code:

public char SampleValue
{
*   get { return samplevalue; }*
}

The name and data type of the property are identical to those of the member variable. You just have to type the first letter in uppercase. Properties don't have parentheses, so you can't consider them as methods. The "get" part inside a property retrieves the data inside your member variable.

When you create an object that belongs to the "Character" class, your computer will generate a variable called "samplevalue". The characters used in the program have two possible forms: uppercase and lowercase. If the value of the character is equal to that of the variable, the former will be an illegal object. The character will be legal once your program generates a result. You can solve this problem using a constructor.

Constructors are methods that run automatically during the creation of an object. In C#, you will use a constructor to initialize an instance variable. For the current program, the constructor will generate a result and make sure that your character will have a valid value. Creating an object is easy if you already know the name of the class. To create an object called "character1" in the "Character" class, you should type:

Character character1 = new Character();

Visibility of Class Members

Classes have an attribute called "visibility". In C# programs, a class can be "internal" or "public". The Character class given above is public, which means anyone can generate objects that belong to the Character type. To create an "internal" class, you should use the following syntax:

internal class Sample

You can instantiate this class from classes that have an identical assembly (i.e. exe or dll). The default visibility of C# classes is internal. The objects inside a class, however, are not limited to two visibility types. You can tag a class member as:

- internal
- public
- protected
- private
- protected internal

To keep things simple, let's focus on the internal, public, and private visibility types. An internal member is accessible to all methods that have a similar assembly. A public member is accessible to all methods present in the program. A private member, meanwhile, is accessible to the methods inside its own class. Keep in mind that "type visibility" is more important than "member visibility". Thus, a public member that belongs to an internal class is not accessible to other assemblies.

C# allows you to set the visibility of methods and variables. But most programmers set instance variables as "protected" or "private". These programmers follow the principle of data encapsulation. Basically, this principle states that who created the class should determine the accessibility of that class. To access an instance variable, you have to use the properties and methods of the class where the variable belongs to. In other words, you should use the services offered by the said class.

Important Note: Creating a class object involves the creation of instance variables. In addition, the constructor of the class will run. If there is no constructor, the program will generate a constructor automatically. Constructors created this way don't have any parameter. Remember that constructors are typeless methods that have the class' name.

Chapter 9: Class Designs and Methods

Designing Your Programs

Aside from being a data type, a class also serves as a design plan. Classes set the appearance, memory requirements, and method of creation of C# objects. An object always contains a value: it obtains the value from the class' instant variables. With the help of methods, a class also specifies how you can use, read, or alter the state of an object.

Each C# application contains a group of classes. These classes define the behavior and functions of the program. An active application consists of objects created according to the application's classes. These objects help each other in achieving the current goal of the application. Thus, creating a program means writing classes that will form your desired program. Keep in mind, however, that there are no strict rules regarding the classes that you can use. In fact, you can rewrite the same program using various combinations of classes. The process of determining the best classes for a program is called "designing".

Many programmers assume that the classes themselves are not important as long as the program does what it is supposed to do. However, nothing could be further from the truth. If you used the wrong classes, you might encounter the following problems:

- You won't understand how the program works. Thus, error detection will be difficult.
- Improving and maintaining the program will be complex and time-consuming.

- You won't be able to reuse the classes of that program in your future projects.

Thus, proper design (i.e. accurate selection of classes) plays an important role in programming. Keep in mind that classes are not just data types - they can describe or define complex concepts inside your programs. Don't think of classes as data types. Rather, think of them as tools that can make your programs more powerful.

C# objects have four elements:

- identifier - This element helps you in identifying and referencing an object.
- state - This is the current value of the object.
- behavior - It defines the capabilities of the object.
- life cycle - It specifies the time period in which the object will stay active.

C# Methods

This part of the book will focus on four topics, namely:

- method identifiers
- return values
- properties
- parameters

Let's discuss these topics one by one:

Method Identifiers

Creating an identifier (or name) for a method is easy and simple. The rules are the same as that of naming variables. Thus, you can use numbers and letters when naming a method. But the first character can never be a number. Most C# programmers, however, choose to place an uppercase letter at the start of a method identifier. You can identify a method using its name and parameters. Thus, you can use the same identifier for many methods. You just have to assign different parameters to each method that you'll create. Check the following example:

```
static int Sample (int x, int y)
{
        return x < y ? y : x;
}
static uint Sample (uint x, uint y)
{
        return x < y ? y : x;
}
static int Sample (int x, int y, int z)
{
        return Sample (Sample (x, y), Sample (y, z));
}
```

The C# compiler differentiates methods based on two factors: their names and their parameters. Parameters can have different quantities and/or data types. Remember that you cannot invoke a method just by specifying its name. You also need to indicate the parameters of the method you are referring to.

Return Values

The previous example specifies the return value of each method. If your methods have a return value, they will have a value after their execution. That means you can use a method in your programming expressions (just like variables). Here's an example:

```
uint d = Sample (100, 200);
```

Here, the method's return value will go to the variable named "d". If a method has a return data type, it should always have one return statement. The return statement generates the method's return value, usually through a programming expression. Remember that you can use any data type for your methods' return type. Also, methods can hold single values only.

Important Note: You should use "void" (i.e. a C# keyword) to indicate methods that don't have to generate return values.

Properties

Properties are methods that require a unique syntax. Theoretically, properties can accomplish anything. Most programmers, however, utilize properties to read and/or alter the contents of instance variables. A property is still a method so you should use an uppercase letter as its first character. The following code will illustrate how properties work:

```
class Cartesian
{
        public int a;
        public int b;
        internal Cartesian (int a, int b)
        {
                this.a = a;
                this.b = b;
        }
        internal int A
        {
                get { return a; }
                set { a = value; }
        }
        internal int B
```

```
        {
                get { return b; }
                set { y = value; }
        }
        internal override string ToString()
        {
                return string.Format (" ( { 1 }, { 5 } ) ", a, b);
        }
}
```

This class can represent specific points in the Cartesian plane. The "a" variable refers to the horizontal axis while the "b" variable refers to the vertical axis. The provided coordinates are internal, which means you can't access them from other assemblies. To access these coordinates, you should use the "get" property. If you want to modify the entries, you must also use the "set" property.

Parameters

The parameters of a method can belong to any data type. While defining a method, you should specify its parameters. These parameters, known as "formal parameters", set the values that your method will use. While calling a method, you have to specify the parameters (or values) that must be given to that method. Programmers refer to these values as "actual parameters".

The Value Parameters

The parameters you will encounter are likely to be value parameters. Check the following code:

```
static uint Sample (uint x, uint y)
{
        return x < y ? y : x;
}
```

Invoking this method involves the transmission of two parameters. While calling a method, the system generates an activation block on the computer's stack. An activation block consists of the following:

- A duplicate of the actual parameters
- The program's return address
- A spot for the program's return value
- The local variables of the method, if any

When your program invokes the "Sample" method, the former will generate one activation block on the computer's stack. The activation block will copy the method's actual parameters and return address. Then, the method will perform its functions. Keep in mind that the method's work applies to the copied arguments only. That means the modifications done by the method won't affect your program. Once the return statement executes, the resulting value will go to the activation block and the method will stop. The program will continue what it was doing before. Also, the computer will delete the method's activation block from the stack of the computer.

Check the following method:

```
internal void Swap (uint x, uint y)
{
        uint z = x;
        x = y;
        y = z;
}
```

This method switches the values inside the "x" and "y" parameters. Testing the Swap() method, however, shows that the reversal doesn't happen on the parameters. Here's the code:

```
static void Test()
{
        uint z1 = 3;
        uint z2 = 4;
        Swap (z1, z2);
        Console.WriteLine ("{ 1 } { 2 } ", z1, z2);
}
```

The Reference Parameters

The .NET framework allows you to use reference parameters in your programs. Let's rewrite the Swap() method discussed earlier:

```
internal void Swap (ref uint x, ref uint y)
{
        uint z = x;
        x = y;
        y = z;
}
```

Now, you can rewrite the Test() method this way:

```
static void Test()
{
        uint z1 = 3;
        uint z2 = 4;
        Swap (ref z1, ref z2);
        Console.WriteLine ("{ 1 } { 2 }", z1, z2);
}
```

With this code, your parameters point to the ones at the top of the computer stack. Also, the Swap() method switches the values inside the z1 and z2 variables. Thus, the changes performed by the method will also affect the parameters it is pointing to.

Important Note: C# programmers use reference parameters when they have to reflect the results of a method on the invoking code. However, C# allows you to combine value and reference parameters in a single method.

The "Out" Parameters

The .NET framework also supports "out parameters". An out parameter gets its value from the method. You can't initialize this parameter before invoking a method. In the code given below, two objects point to the method's out parameters:

```
static void Cartesian2(int a1, int b1, int a2, int b2, out
Cartesian d1, out Point d2)
{
        d1 = new Cartesian (a1, b1);
        d2 = new Cartesian (a2, b2);
}
```

If you will execute the Cartesian2 method this way:

```
static void Test()
{
        Cartesian d1;
        Cartesian d2;
        Cartesian2 (3, 6, 8, 4, out d1, out d2);
        Console.WriteLine (d1);
        Console.WriteLine (d2);
}
```

d1 and d2 point to the class objects created by the Cartesian2() method. As you can see, you didn't initialize d1 and d2 within the program. This approach works because you used the said parameters as "out" parameters. Methods cannot hold multiple return values. But you can overcome this limitation using out parameters.

The Default Parameters

C# lets you create default parameters in your programs. Analyze the following code:

```
static float Compute (float price, int unit = 1, float discounts = 3)
{
        return price * unit * (100 - discounts) / 100;
}
```

This method computes the discounted price of a product. The default number of units is 1, while the default discount rate is 3%. Thus, you can invoke the Compute() method without indicating the values of "unit" and "discounts". Here's an example:

```
static void Test()
{
        Console.WriteLine (Compute (1000) );
        Console.WriteLine (Compute (1000, 10) );
        Console.WriteLine (Compute (1000, 20) );
}
```

The program will use the default values if actual numbers don't exist.

Chapter 10: Class Inheritance

At this point, you should know how important classes are in creating your own C# programs. Be careful when checking and/or editing an existing class, because one undesirable change can lead to serious (also known as "fatal") errors. However, there are situations where you have to add more properties into your current classes. C# supports "inheritance", a feature that allows you to extend classes without affecting the original ones. Inheritance is also useful in situations where you have to create almost identical classes. You can just create the shared attributes in a "parent" class and have "children" classes inherit from it.

The code given below will show you the syntax of class inheritance:

```
public class Sample
{
        public int a;
        public int b;

        public Sample (int a, int b)
        {
                this.a = a;
                this.b = b;
        }
        public int A
        {
                get { return a; }
                set { a = value; }
        }

        public int B
        {
                get { return b; }
```

```
                set { b = value; }
        }
        internal override string ToString()
        {
                return string.Format ("({ 1 }, { 2 })", a, b);
        }
}
```

This is a basic class, so explanations are not needed. Let's just use this class as the parent of new classes. As you will see, the inheriting classes are improved versions of the original one. For now, let's add a new method to the class:

```
public class SampleChild : Sample
{
        public SampleChild (int a, int b) : base (a, b)
        {
        }
        internal void Add (Sample s)
        {
                A += s.A;
                B += s.B;
        }
}
```

To create an inheriting class, you should use the following syntax:

```
public class NewClass : ParentClass
```

The inheriting class copies or improves the contents of the parent class. Thus, the child class will have two sets of contents: (1) the objects and methods from the original class, and (2) the methods and objects you'll define during class declaration (if any). This feature is extremely useful - you can enhance a class without affecting it permanently. Rather than modifying your original class, you can just duplicate it and work on the new files.

While creating an object in the "child" class, the class will send values to its "parent". You can accomplish it by inserting the "base" keyword after the class constructor. The program given below utilizes the SampleChild class created earlier:

```
static void (Main(string[] args)
{
        SampleChild s1 = new SampleChild (3, 4);
        SampleChild s2 = new SampleChild ( 2, 5);
        s1.Add (s2);
        s1.A = s1.A * 4;
        Console.WriteLine (s1);
}
```

Let's use a more complex example:

```
public class Individual
{
        private string name1;
        private string name2;

        public Player (string name1, string name2)
        {
                this.name1 = name1;
                this.name2 = name2;
        }

        public string Name1
        {
                get { return name1; }
        }
        public string Name2
        {
```

```
            get { return name2; }
    }

    internal override string ToString()
    {
            return name1 + " " + name2;
    }
}
```

This class represents an individual. Here, name1 refers to the person's first name. Meanwhile, name2 refers to the last name. Let's use this class to create another one. The next class has two new properties: the title of the player and his age. You can write the second class in different ways. But the easiest way involves inheriting information from the "Individual" class created earlier. Here's the code:

Note: This program (like the previous ones) uses chess-related terms.

```
public class Player : Individual
{
        private string title;
        private int age;

        public Player (string name1, string name2, string
title, int age)
                : base (name1, name2)
        {
                this.title = title;
                this.age = age;
        }
        public string Title
        {
                get { return title; }
        }
        public int Age
```

```
        {
                get { return age; }
        }

        internal override string ToString()
        {
                return base.ToString() + "\n" + title;
        }
}
```

The first line informs the language compiler that "Player" will inherit data from "Individual". Thus, the Player class will copy (i.e. inherit) the properties present in the Individual class and add new ones. The inheriting class contains a constructor. This constructor creates two new variables: title and age. It should also initialize the variables from the original class (i.e. the name1 and name2 variables). You can't invoke the parent class directly, so you have to use the following statement:

```
: base (name1, name2)
```

Now, let's create another class. This one will inherit the information inside "Player". Let's use "WorldChampion" as the name of the new class. Basically, it adds a new property to the existing data (i.e. it says whether the player became a chess world champion).

```
public class WorldChampion : Player
{
        public WorldChampion (string name1, string name2,
int age)
                : base (name1, name2, "WorldChampion",
age)
        {
        }
}
```

Important Note: The main point behind this example is that you can use a "child" class as the "parent" of a new class.

Chapter 11: The Object Class

All classes are "child" classes. Even your first class inherits some data from an older one. In particular, all C# classes inherit information from a built-in class named "Object". Additionally, this is the parent of any data type that you can use (i.e. whether it's a reference or value type).

The C# language uses the word "object" as an alias for the "System.Object" class. C# does the same thing for other built-in classes, such as "string" for "System.String".

The "Object" class doesn't offer anything special. Its main goal is to serve as the parent class for any type or class that you will ever use. This class contains some useful methods. Let's discuss these methods one by one:

```
class Player
{
        private string completeName;
        private string currentElo;

        public Player (string completeName, string
currentElo)
        {
                this.completeName = completeName;
                this.currentElo = currentElo;
        }

        public string CompleteName
        {
                get { return completeName }
        }

        public string currentElo
        {
```

```
        get { return currentElo; }
    }
}
```

By default, the Player class is a child of the "Object" class. Analyze the method given below:

```
static void Test()
{
        Player a = new Player ("Anish Giri", "2767");
        Console.WriteLine (a);
}
```

This code creates an object that belongs to the "Player" type. In addition, the content of the new object will appear on your command prompt. Keep in mind that WriteLine() uses the ToString() method complete its task. The Player class doesn't have its own ToString() method, but you can still translate and execute the program. Here, the ToString() comes from System.Object. That means all C# objects have a corresponding ToString() method.

You can also use the Equals() method in your C# programs. Basically, Equals() checks whether your parameter and an object are identical. It will give you "True" if the objects are identical; otherwise, it will give you "False". Check the following code:

```
static void Test()
{
        Player a1 = new Player ("Anish Giri", "2767");
        Player a2 = new Player ("Anish Giri", "2767");
        Console.WriteLine (a1.Equals (a2) );
}
```

If you will run this code, you will receive "False". That is not surprising. The objects you are checking (i.e. a1 and a2) contain identical values, but they are pointing to different objects. Note that the Equals() method compares references. Since a1 and a2 refer to different objects, the Test() code given above will result to "False". It doesn't matter whether the values are the same. But C# allows you to override the said behavior. You can rewrite the previous code as:

```
public override bool Equals(object obj)
{
        if (obj is Player)
        {
                Player a = (Player) obj;
                return completeName.Equals
(a.completeName) && currentElo.Equals (a.currentElo);
        }
        return false;
}
```

You can use "is" (a C# operator) to check the data type of an object. The Equals() method will give you "True" only if "obj" belongs to the same type as "Player".

Chapter 12: The Abstract Classes

This chapter will focus on abstract classes. An abstract class can serve as the parent of other classes. However, you can't instantiate it or create objects under it. The example given below will show you the syntax of abstract classes:

```
internal abstract class Sample
{
        private int a;
        private int b;

        public Sample (int a, int b)
        {
                this.a = a;
                this.b = b;
        }
        public int A
        {
                get { return A; }
                set { a = value; }
        }
        public int B
        {
                get { return b; }
                set { b = value; }
        }

        internal override string ToString()
        {
                return string.Format("( { 1 }, { 2 }", a, b);
        }

        internal abstract void Test();
        internal abstract void Check();
}
```

The last part of this code generates abstract methods, namely Test() and Check(). These methods don't have any code, so you can consider them as useless definitions. As the programmer, you know that they exist but you can't use them. Additionally, the entire class is an abstract one. It simply means that you cannot generate objects that belong to the "Sample" type.

Let's create a class that inherits "Sample". Now, the abstract methods will serve an actual purpose:

```
internal class NewSample : Sample
{
        public NewSample (int a, int b) : base (a, b)
        {
        }

        internal override void Test()
        {
                --A;
                --B;
        }

        internal override void Check()
        {
                ++A;
                ++B;
        }
}
```

Important Note: You should use the keyword "override" before abstract methods in inheriting classes.

The Main() method given below utilizes the NewSample class:

```
static void Main(string[] args)
{
        Sample r = new NewSample (3, 4);
        Console.WriteLine (r);
        r.Test();
        Console.WriteLine (r);
        r.Check();
        Console.WriteLine (r);
}
```

Chapter 13: The Interfaces of the C# Language

Abstract classes are data types that may hold all the properties (e.g. methods, variables, constructors, etc.) of a typical class. Interfaces, on the other hand, are data types that can hold abstract methods only. Let's illustrate this concept using a basic example:

```
public interface InterfaceSample
{
        int A { get; set; }
        int B { get; set; }
}
```

The code given above is similar to an ordinary class. The only difference is that it includes the "interface" keyword. You can use this keyword to define properties and methods. Keep in mind that interfaces can only hold abstract methods. In addition, the resulting methods are automatically tagged as "public".

You can implement the said interface using the following class:

```
public class Sample : InterfaceSample
{
        private int a;
        private int b;

        public Sample (int a, int b)
        {
                this.a = a;
                this.b = b;
        }
```

```
public int A
{
        get { return a; }
        set { a = value; }
}

public int B
{
        get { return b; }
        set { b = value; }
}

internal override string ToString()
{
        return string.Format(" ( { 1 }, { 2 } ) ", a, b);
}
}
```

This code uses the syntax for typical inheritance:

public class Sample : InterfaceSample

When you implement an interface inside a class, the class should adopt all of the methods and properties inside the interface. Check the following Main() method:

```
static void Main(string[] args)
{
        InterfaceSample r = new Sample (3, 4);
        Console.WriteLine (r);
}
```

Chapter 14: The Static Members

Now, let's focus on the static contents of a class. In C#, you can create a static method or variable. Actually, this language allows you to create static classes.

When creating an object, you have to generate information elements as ordinary variables. If there are other objects inside the class, you must represent them using instance variables. All objects inside the class have a copy of the instance variables. If an object will alter its instance variables, other objects won't be affected.

But static variables are different. You should create static variables while creating a class object. That means each object inside a class will share the same static variable. Keep in mind that static variables are not linked to any specific object.

Random number generators serve as an excellent example for this. The said generators belong to the "Random" data type. You have to initialize the generator while declaring a static variable. Here's an example:

public static Random sample = new Random();

The process described above is not mandatory. In fact, it can be undesirable (or impossible) at times. As an alternative, you can use a constructor to initialize your static variables. This kind of constructor is called "static constructor". The following example will show you how static constructors work:

public class Sample
{
        public static Random sample;

```
        public int fdgop;

        static Sample()
        {
                sample = new Random();
        }
}
```

Creating Static Methods

You can use static methods without any class object. When referencing a static method, you should indicate the class identifier before the method's name.

Writing a Program

In this part of the book, you will create a program that relies on static methods. It has a class that contain methods for string manipulation. Thus, you can use this class in many situations. Here is the code:

```
internal static class StringClass
        {
        internal static string Cutter(string content, long
widthchecker)
        {
                if (content.Length > widthchecker) return
content.Substring (0, widthchecker);
                return content;
        }

        internal static string FilltoRight(string content, long
widthchecker, char character)
        {
                StringBuilder sample = new StringBuilder
(content);
```

```
            while (sample.Length < widthchecker)
sample.Append (character);
            return sample.ToString();
      }
      internal static string FilltoLeft(string content, long
widthchecker, char character)
      {
            if (content.Length >= widthchecker) return
content;
            StringBuilder sample = new StringBuilder
(widthchecker - content.Length);
            for (long x = 0; x < sample.Capacity; ++x)
sample.Append (character);
            return sample.ToString() + content;
      }


      internal static string FilltoCenter(string content, long
widthchecker, char character)
      {
            return FilltoRight (FilltoLeft (content,
content.Length + (widthchecker - content.Length) / 2,
character), widthchecker, character);
      }
}
```

Chapter 15: Data Types

The C# language supports different data types, such as interface and class types. As mentioned earlier in the book, there are two major categories of data types: value and reference.

Variables that belong to the value type assigns stack space for their data. Thus, you may think that these variables contain their own data. All of these variables will self-destruct (i.e. disappear from the computer's stack) as soon as your program stops using them.

Variables of the reference type, on the other hand, don't have information inside them. Rather, they just point to data found on the computer's heap. That means multiple reference variables can point to a single object. Also, all reference variables are four bytes in size. If you don't want a reference point to point to anything, you may set its value as "null". You can divide reference types into three groups: arrays, classes, and interface.

The ValueType Struct

The basic data types of C# come from the ValueType struct. This struct, in turn, originates from the built-in class named "Object". You can divide basic types into the following categories:

- bool
- char
- integer types

- decimal types

The "bool" data type has two possible values: True and False. This is the perfect type for conditional expressions. The "char" type, meanwhile, represents characters as 16-bit codes. Keep in mind that this data type relies on a character system called "Unicode". Use the integer data types when you are dealing with whole numbers. The decimal types, as their name indicate, are perfect for numbers with fractional or decimal part.

Important Note: Structs are type declarations that define a collection of variables.

Conclusion

I hope this book was able to help you master the basics of C# programming. The tips, tricks, and techniques you found in this book can aid you in becoming a skilled C# programmer.

The next step is to read more books about C#. This computer language involves more advanced concepts. Don't settle for the basics. If you are serious about programming, strive to learn more about your craft. In addition, continue writing your own codes. This way, you will be able to apply your knowledge.

Finally, if you enjoyed this book, please take the time to share your thoughts and post a review on Amazon. It'd be greatly appreciated!

Thank you and good luck!